WHAT TO DO IF YOU ARE IN A
CAR ACCIDENT
IN
WASHINGTON STATE

The Seven Absolutely Essential Steps
You Must Take To Get The Money You
Deserve And Get Back To Normal

By Matthew T. Russell and James V. Hill
Attorneys At Law

Prepared For Publication by Jesse Stoddard

Publisher: Stoddard Productions

ISBN: 9781790881475

Printed in the United States of America

Who are we at Russell & Hill? We are your neighbors, friends, coaches, and the people you meet in your stores, local parks, and communities. We are hardworking, family-orientated professionals who care about our clients and are committed to making a difference in their lives. We are skilled and experienced at trial and handle complex litigation cases.

At Russell & Hill, we organize our firm to make it as easy as possible for you to consult an attorney about your legal problem. We understand that most people do not speak to attorneys until something bad has happened. We believe talking to a lawyer should not add to the stress of your situation. Instead, it should be the first step on the road to resolving your legal issue as quickly and effectively as possible. If you need an experienced, caring attorney in the Pacific Northwest, give us a call.

If you have been in an automobile collision and are in need of legal advice, we would love to offer you a free no-pressure legal consultation. Simply visit us at **www.RussellandHill.com** or call **1-800-LAW-0842** for a free consultation.

Sincerely,
Matt Russell & Jim Hill

Dedication

To our spouses and children, who gracefully put up with our

long hours and demanding careers.

Table of Contents

Chapter 6: Getting Compensation By Using A Strong Demand Package **58**

Chapter 7: Post Settlement—What To Do After The Dust Settles 70

Conclusion **75**

Glossary of Terms   77

Acknowledgments

This book, the many people we help, and work we do in general, would not be possible without the amazing attorneys, paralegals, and support staff at Russell & Hill, PLLC. Thank you Brandon Batchelor, Eric Bessent, Amy Brown, Dustin K Burk, Jaclyn J. Gaddy, Dean Swanson, Diana Smith, Jill MacInnes, Gabriela Carninschi, Tina Carey, Kim Knutson, Kris Michaud, Elizabeth Nyambura, Alice Gerke, Kristen Hill, Michelle Moen, and Dradin Kreft. Thank you to our diligent editor Jesse Stoddard and his hard-working assistant Ryan Trimble for their work in interviewing and preparing this book for publication.

Preface

Who is this book for?

If you've been in a car crash, this book is for you. Trying to deal with insurance companies, medical care providers, and the trauma of being in a collision can be overwhelming. Navigating insurance claims can be a very complicated and daunting process, and it can be easy to make costly mistakes. Insurance companies will often try to take advantage of you because of this, so we want to help you before it's too late.

How can this book help you?

This book will give you information on what to look out for after being in a collision. We will offer advice on dealing with your medical care, handling your medical bills, and even how to interact with insurance companies, so you can be properly compensated in your claim. You will learn about documentation, how to handle damage to your vehicle, what to do if you end up in the emergency room, and when to go to your primary care physician. We discuss how your medical expenses will be paid, and how to ensure you are properly compensated. We even help you figure out what to do after your claim is finished and settled. We want to take away your anxiety and provide you with the justice you deserve.

If I get injured, when do I need an attorney?

You should find an attorney as soon as possible after the collision. There are so many ways your claim can go wrong in the first few days. It is incredibly important to have excellent guidance right from the start. If you do not hire an attorney right away, you should contact them when you start to realize something is not quite right. Trust your instincts. If you are on the phone with an insurance adjuster, you might get the feeling they are putting you on the defensive or are looking for ways to use facts against you, even if you cannot articulate how. When you get that feeling, trust your intuition and call an attorney; they will help answer your questions whether you hire them or not. You will be less stressed and you will get the most value out of your attorney if you put them to work early. It is also important to recall that the attorneys at Russell & Hill do not get paid until your claim is resolved. Our attorneys get paid the same whether you hire them one day after your collision or one year. So, you might as well put us to work for you as soon as you can.

If I get injured, how do I find a good attorney?

The first step is usually searching the internet. Look for professional websites and firms with good reviews and ratings. Look for testimonials. It's also a good idea to ask family and friends; they might have experience with a firm and steer you in the right direction. Once you have narrowed down your list, you should interview your top choices. It is important to personally get along well with your attorneys and be able to work together with them. You must trust your attorneys. You want to be sure that you are comfortable with whom you pick because you could be working with them for months, or even years.

What should I look for in a personal injury attorney?

You should look for commitment and experience. You don't want to go to someone who is inexperienced in personal injury because it is too complex of an area of law. You want someone who specializes in these types of cases and has years of experience under their belt. You want someone who has seen it all.

Also, it is important that your attorney is willing to go to trial. Many attorneys will not go to trial because it is expensive, time-consuming, and risky. Some attorneys do not want to go simply because they are afraid to. The insurance companies know which personal injury attorneys go to trial and those who do not. Because of this, insurance companies will not offer those attorneys the best settlement for you. But an attorney who is willing to go to trial and means business will get the best offers from insurance companies prior to litigation. So choose an attorney who has a reputation of going to trial to get the outcome you deserve.

Your attorney also needs to be a good communicator. They need to be able to communicate with you, the insurance companies, and other parties in the case. You want to be able to call their office and get a meeting in any form that you need, whether it's a phone or video call, email, or coming into the office and sitting down face to face. Two things that indicate a good legal team is prompt responses to your emails or phone calls and a well-staffed office. A well-staffed firm will take care of you. Remember, you and your attorneys are a team, and a team functions best with good communication.

A note on insurance companies

Insurance companies are profit-driven organizations. They make money by taking in insurance premiums and refusing to pay claims, even rightful ones. Insurance companies make money by finding ways to deny your claim. It does not matter if it is your own insurance company or the insurance company for a person who has injured you. It does not matter if you have been a customer of your insurance company for 30 years and have not made a single claim. The insurance industry survives by taking in money and refusing to pay claims.

The worst offenders are the major car insurance companies like Geico, State Farm, Farmers, etc. These companies will use every possible avenue to destroy your claim. They are given every advantage to do so. They have nearly unlimited resources. They are allowed to hide from the jury while in the courtroom. These companies, through their attorneys and employees, will lie, cheat, and steal their way to a victory in the courtroom. Unfortunately, they are all too often successful in doing so. Insurance companies are not your friend, they are not equitable, they do not care about you. You are not in "good hands" while dealing with your insurance company.

Insurance companies know that most people are not used to dealing with the issues discussed in this book. Insurance companies take advantage of every misstep an injured person may make to avoid paying compensation. Because of this, you need skilled litigators like the attorneys at Russell & Hill.

How much will it cost me to hire a personal injury attorney?

At Russell & Hill, it will not cost you anything up front. We understand you likely do not have thousands of dollars to throw at a case from the beginning. You are already a victim in a collision, and we do not want to add burden to you. We will work with you on a contingency fee, rather than an hourly fee, meaning we get paid at the end of the claim when we achieve a settlement for you. A contingency fee allows our interests to be the same as yours. When we procure a proper resolution of your claim, we are paid. Our motivations are directly aligned with yours.

So how much does your attorney cost? Nothing.

Now that you have a good handle on how this book is going to help you relieve some of the stress of being injured through the fault of someone else, and how to get the right help from a good law firm, let's take a look at the critical first steps to take when you are in a collision, including one of the most crucial and overlooked areas of the process: documentation.

Chapter 1: Help! I've Been In A Car Crash! What Now?

In this chapter, we are going to cover the most pressing questions people have immediately following a collision, including the information-gathering process, police and incident reports, what to do about the other person's insurance, at-the-scene documentation, if and when you need to call the police, what to file within 48 hours, and whether you should make any statements to other parties involved in the collision. More importantly, we are going to discuss how you can get all these things taken care of early so you do not run into trouble later.

Who do I call after my collision?

First, call 911. If you cannot call, get a bystander to call. A police officer needs to come to the scene and make a police report so you can be sure everything is properly documented. Make sure pictures are taken of the damage to vehicles, as well as their position and orientation to each other.

If you are able, take pictures of the licenses and insurance information of the other people involved in the collision. This will be the easiest way to make sure you have all the information necessary to reach the other parties involved in the collision if need be.

If you are injured, go to the doctor. If need be, ask for an ambulance to take you to the emergency room. You can also call a loved one to let them know what happened, and have them take you to get medical care. If you are injured at all, it is best to seek professional medical assistance as soon as possible.

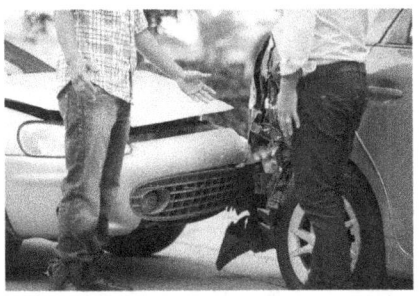

Should I talk about the collision at the scene?

We recommend that you only speak to police officers about what happened in the collision or how you feel. Do not discuss "fault" with the person who hit you or the witnesses. If you speak to witnesses, get their contact information and ask what they saw. If you speak to other drivers involved in the collision, get their contact and insurance information. If the person that hit you is hostile to you, which happens sometimes, we recommend taking a video of that person on your mobile phone.

When is it appropriate to leave the scene versus staying until the police get there?

Ideally, you should always stay and wait for the police to arrive. In some circumstances, the police will not respond to a collision. A 911 dispatcher will let you know whether police are coming.

If the police do not come to the collision, you will need to gather documentation on your own. Take photos of license plates, insurance cards, and driver's licenses, if possible. Also get the names and contact information of any witnesses.

Then, you can go to the police station and file a report yourself. Under Washington Law, you must file a police report within four days of the incident. However, some insurance policies require you to file a police report within 48 hours if no police came to the scene, so be on the safe side and file your report within 48 hours.

Should I call an insurance agent or an attorney?

Call your insurance agent first to open a claim. This will help expedite the repair of the car and help you get a rental car sooner. They can also tell you if you have Personal Injury Protection (PIP) so you can schedule a doctor's appointment. Then call an attorney so they can help advise you on your claim and your next steps.

How do I get a police report?

Call your attorney first, they can get one the fastest. Otherwise, you can make a Public Records Request or go to the police station and request one directly.

Typically, we can get a police report the same day we order it. It usually takes longer for you to get one on your own. If you schedule a consultation to discuss your claim, we can get a copy of the police report for free. As officers of the court, we also have access to the Judicial Information System (JIS), where we can look up if the other driver has been cited previously, was involved in other collisions, and other information about the collision.

If my car was towed, what do I do?

If your car was towed, get it out of the tow yard as soon as possible. Tow yards charge daily storage fees, so you want to keep those costs as low as possible. Call the other driver's insurance company and let them know your car is there; they will typically get it out of the tow yard themselves so they do not rack up daily storage fees. If the other insurance company will not assist you, contact your own insurance or contact your attorney immediately. This is also something we can assist with.

Can I go to any auto body repair shop that I please?

Yes, under Washington law, you can take your vehicle to an auto body repair shop of your choosing. If you're going to have your car fixed, it is best to work with the insurance company of the person that caused the collision (the at-fault driver). If you go through your own insurance company, you may get penalized with higher insurance rates for simply being in the collision. You would also have to pay your deductible to get the vehicle repaired, although your attorney can get that money repaid to you. The at-fault party's insurance might recommend that you go to one of their preferred repair shops. We do *not* recommend you follow their advice. We recommend you get opinions from three different shops of your own choosing in order to make sure nothing is missed, and you have a good idea of what the repairs will cost. Your attorneys can make recommendations on which repair shops to go to as well.

How do I get my car repaired if the other insurance company says they won't fix it?

If you have collision coverage on your policy, your insurance will help you pay for it. However, you will have to pay your deductible. If at all possible, it is best to go through the at-fault driver's insurance. Sometimes, the other insurance provider will not pay for the damage to your car because they do not want to admit fault for the collision until they have spoken to the driver. It could take weeks for them to act if they do not have anyone pushing them to reach a decision. If that is the case, you should get an attorney, to assist in getting your car repaired.

Who pays my deductible?

If you make a claim through your own insurance company to have your car repaired, you have to pay your deductible, but you will be repaid once it is determined that the other driver was at fault. If the at-fault driver's insurance admits their driver was at fault, you will not have to pay your deductible.

Can I get a rental car?

Typically you can if you had rental car coverage as part of your insurance policy at the time of the collision. The at-fault party will also allow for a rental car until your vehicle is fixed or your car is determined a total loss (totaled).

Can I get a rental car if it is not covered in my insurance?

Yes, you can. If neither of the insurance companies will pay for a rental car, you can pay for it yourself upfront, and we can get it reimbursed later if you had the rental car for a reasonable amount of time. Be diligent in getting your car fixed or getting into a new car as soon as possible because it is difficult to get reimbursed for the rental car if you had it for an unnecessarily long period of time.

Who pays my medical bills?

If your insurance has Personal Injury Protection (PIP) coverage, that coverage will pay for your medical bills, deductibles, and other costs up to the amount specified in your coverage, usually $10,000 dollars. PIP is great to have on your policy because it is relatively inexpensive, and there are no copays or deductibles. You can find out if you have PIP coverage by calling your agent, or by looking at the declarations page of your insurance policy. If you have PIP coverage, that coverage is considered the first coverage to be used in any injury claim. So even if you have great health insurance, they will not pay anything until your PIP coverage has been exhausted.

Once you use up all of your PIP coverage, that is when it is time to go to your own health insurance provider. They will need a letter from PIP stating the coverage is exhausted. If you do not have PIP coverage at all, then you will have to go directly through your health insurance provider. You must pay your deductibles and copays to your health insurance until your claim is resolved.

If you do not have PIP or health insurance, you will have to pay out of pocket for your medical expenses. Most people cannot afford to pay for medical treatment out of pocket. We can help you find doctors, physical therapists, and chiropractors who will treat you and hold the bills until your claim is settled.

Should I talk to the adjuster that's calling me?

You have a duty to speak with the adjuster from your own insurance company. You have no duty to speak with the at-fault driver's insurance company and we recommend you do *not* communicate with the at-fault driver's insurance company unless it is about vehicle damage only. Do *not* answer questions about how the collision happened (liability), your injuries, or how you're doing. The at-fault driver's insurance company will pressure you to give them information, so that information can be later used to avoid compensating you. The only information you should discuss is vehicle damage.

What is an example of a legitimate vehicle damage question they might ask that I should talk to them about?

The at-fault driver's insurance company may ask "Where is your car located? We want to take a look at it and work on getting it fixed for you. In the meantime, we will give you a rental car." Alternatively, they may say something like this: "What kind of options did your car have, did it have any accessories?" These are safe questions to answer. However, be prepared for a follow-up question like "I'm sorry to hear about your collision, how are you feeling?" Do not answer questions like that, because your answer could be used against you in court. Respond by saying, "I'll be going to the doctor. I'll let you know how I'm feeling when I'm done treating." You are not obligated to work with the at-fault driver's insurance, but if they are going to repair or replace your car, you should work with the vehicle damage adjuster to get fair value for your vehicle.

Do I give a statement to the at-fault driver's insurance company?

Absolutely not! If they ask for a statement, call an attorney. They are looking for things to use against you and want a recording from you they can use in Court. They know you may simply forget to give them information about *all* your injuries, allowing them to later claim "your neck did not hurt when we first spoke, yet here you are claiming significant neck pain and bills from your doctor." They know how to ask very leading questions that can be interpreted in their favor at a later time. Even when talking to your own insurance, it is best to have the advice of an attorney. You do not want to inadvertently say something that could be held against you. Remember—insurance companies are not your friend. They will use tricks and deceit in order to avoid reasonable compensation for your injuries.

What do I do if the insurance company doesn't respond to my calls?

Call an attorney; they will be able to get a response and help you with your claim.

What are the at-fault driver's insurance policy limits?

Each insurance policy covers damages only up to a certain dollar figure. This is known as the policy limits. The insurance adjuster for the at-fault driver is under no duty to tell you policy limits until a lawsuit has been filed. Likely they will not give you this information. However, your attorney may have a good working relationship with the adjuster, and the adjuster may give hints to your attorney as to the policy limits amount, or at least a specific range the limits may fall within.

Now that you understand the key actions you need to take in order to properly document the process immediately following a collision, we are going to tackle the most common insurance questions so that you can file a vehicle damage claim and get your car fixed or replaced.

Chapter 2: How To Deal With Insurance And Get Your Car Fixed

In this chapter we are going to cover getting your car fixed, getting a rental vehicle, and address the general question of who pays what and for how long. The first step is to open up a property (vehicle) damage claim.

What if they won't give me fair value for my car?

The first thing you should do is ask for the insurance company's valuation report. This report lists the asking price of vehicles that were found online or at a local car dealership and are of a similar make, model, year, etc. You can use this report to determine if the offer is accurate and fair. If you don't think the insurance company's offer is fair, we can recommend experts who will look at your car and give you another estimate of value, which can then be presented to the insurance adjuster and used to argue for an increase in the offer.

Who pays if I owe more on my car than it's worth?

If you have Gap insurance, it will cover the difference between what you owe on your car and what it is actually worth. If you are unsure whether or not you have this type of insurance, look at your purchase documents from the dealership where you bought the vehicle. This coverage may also be listed on your automobile insurance policy. If you don't have Gap insurance you will need to make up the difference on your own. However, keep in mind that a skilled attorney may help with this burden by negotiating a fair injury settlement for you. A good settlement on the injury portion of your claim may help ease the financial burden of having to pay out on the value of your total loss vehicle.

Who pays my deductible?

The at-fault driver will reimburse you for your deductible if you use your insurance company to pay for the repair to your vehicle. If you work through the at-fault driver's insurance company, there will be no deductible. Bear in mind, however, that the at-fault driver's insurance company will not pay for your vehicle damage until they have made a liability determination. If they take too long to make a determination, or if they determine that liability is split and thus only offer a portion of your total damages, you would be best off using your own insurance company to fix your car and pay the deductible. Again, if the at-fault party's insurance decides later that they were, in fact, responsible for the collision, you will be reimbursed.

Which insurance company is easiest to work with?

Usually, we find that the at-fault driver's insurance will give you a fair value because they are very well regulated by state law and also don't want to go through the hassle of haggling back and forth. But typically your own insurance company is easier to work with because they have a greater legal duty to you.

Will my rates go up if I have my insurance pay the vehicle damage?

The answer is *it depends*. Every insurance company has their own guidelines in which they do business. We are aware of some insurance companies who will raise your premium when you let them know you were in an accident by reporting a property damage claim. This is true even when you were not at fault or if nothing was paid out on a claim. However, *most* insurance companies will not raise your premiums unless you are found to be over 50% at fault for the collision.

You or your attorney can review your insurance policy to determine what guidelines your insurance company follows. This is another important reason to get your attorney on the case early.

Who pays for a rental vehicle?

The at-fault driver's insurance will pay for a rental vehicle for just the time that your car is unavailable to you. If they don't, you can have your own insurance company pay for it, if it's on your policy. Sometimes your insurance will only cover a certain cost per day for the rental car, so if you need something bigger or better, you will have to pay the difference out of pocket. If you must pay for a rental car out of pocket, reimbursement for the rental can be sought as a part of your injury claim settlement.

How long can I be in my rental car?

You can continue using your rental car until your car is fixed or the offer to replace it has been given to you. We can often extend that time period to give you a few more days to try to find a vehicle to purchase.

Who pays for items like car seats, phones, and other valuables that were damaged in the collision?

The at-fault driver will reimburse you for those expenses. But in the meantime, you can always use the comprehensive part of your own insurance policy, if you have it. We suggest you first try to use the at-fault driver's insurance so you don't have to worry about any deductibles.

 ## Can I cash a vehicle damage check?

Absolutely, but the insurance company is going to want you to sign a document which releases your vehicle damage claim. You should only sign it if you are comfortable with the amount of money that they are giving you for your vehicle. If you're uncomfortable, don't sign the release document or cash the check until you talk to an attorney.

Will the insurance company total my vehicle?

It depends on the amount of damage. If the cost of fixing the vehicle exceeds 80 percent of what the vehicle is worth, they will total it and present to you an offer that should reflect the actual value of the vehicle at the time of the collision.

You will have the opportunity to "buy back" the totaled vehicle for salvage value. If you choose this option, the insurance company will deduct the salvage value from your total loss offer, and you can keep the vehicle. Be aware that the vehicle's title will carry with it an indication that it has been salvaged. The "salvage title" will significantly lower the value of the vehicle. However, if the damage is mostly cosmetic, or you can fix the car yourself, you can buy the vehicle back from the insurance company for around 10-15% of the valuation price.

Do I have to take my car to the shop the insurance company told me to?

No, you can take it to any shop. We recommend you take it to multiple independent shops to be sure you get a fair estimate of the damage. The insurance companies often have recommendations for repair shops. They might make it seem that you are required to go to the shop they recommend. They are not requirements and you have the right to seek your own automotive experts as well as second opinions.

Where do I take my car to be evaluated or estimated?

Your injury attorney may be able to recommend good auto body shops. We know which shops are working with Geico and State Farm and Allstate (and the other insurance companies), so we can recommend a good independent shop that will give you a fair estimate.

How do I know if I have Gap insurance?

Gap insurance is the difference between the actual cash value of a vehicle and the balance still owed on the financing (car loan, lease, etc.). Gap coverage is mainly used on new and used vehicles (cars and trucks) and heavy trucks. Some financing companies and lease contracts require it. It will be on your car insurance policy, or you could have a separate Gap policy through the dealership where you purchased your vehicle.

We've thoroughly discussed the ins and outs of opening up a vehicle damage claim and dealing with the insurance companies on the vehicle side of things. Now we are going to cover getting proper medical care and how important it is to follow the directions of your doctor if you hope to prevail in your injury claim.

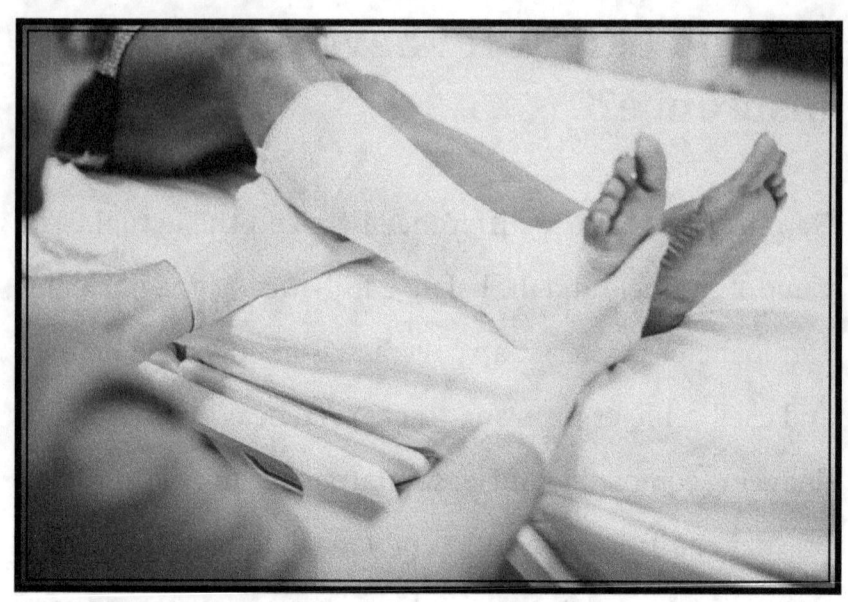

Chapter 3: Going To The ER And Your Primary Care Physician

In this chapter we discuss documenting injuries, getting treatment, and whose advice you need to take seriously if you hope to be reasonably compensated for your injuries.

What do I do for medical treatment and who do I contact?

If you have any acute or sharp pain, go to the ER. You need to find out what's wrong. If it's not severe, an urgent care clinic is a fine option as well, but get in as soon as you can to get treated. If you're not sure, schedule an appointment with your primary care provider. You might not notice something is wrong immediately, so it is important to have a medical professional examine you and diagnose things you may have missed. For example, at the scene of the collision, you might notice that your shoulder is killing you, and miss the fact that your lower back is aching. You might not notice your back until days or weeks later when your shoulder feels better. If you do notice a sharp pain, later on, don't hesitate to go to the ER immediately. If the pain is more subdued, you can go to an urgent care clinic, or schedule an appointment with your doctor.

Do I have to see the care provider that's written on the prescription pad, whether it's a physical therapist, massage therapist, or chiropractor?

You can choose your own health care providers. The referral for the treatment is what's important, and you do not have to see the specific provider that may be printed on a prescription pad. Treatment providers sometimes hand out prescription pads that have their name printed on them for marketing purposes, but again you are not limited to any specific healthcare provider. Find someone you have a relationship with, trust, or get referred to by a trusted source. An additional consideration when choosing treatment providers is insurance coverage. Typically, PIP will cover any provider, while your health insurance may cover only providers within their network.

It's also important that the provider is in a convenient location to you. If it's not convenient, it will make it more difficult to get the care you need. So look for one near your home or on your way home from work. It will be hard enough to schedule 10 to 20 physical therapy appointments around your schedule as it is, so try to make it as easy on yourself as possible.

It's important that you go to all of your prescribed treatments because if you don't, the insurance company can argue that you didn't get better because you didn't follow your doctor's advice and follow through with all of your prescribed treatments.

Should I take the pills prescribed by the doctor?

Yes. You should listen to your doctor and do what they prescribe; otherwise, you are giving the insurance company an argument to use against you. However, keep an open line of communication with your doctor. For instance, if you are worried about prescription drug addiction, let your doctor know about that. They may be able to find alternatives that still work given your needs or concerns. That way you can be comfortable doing what your doctor prescribes, and not give the insurance company an argument to use against you.

Should I get imaging done?

If you have a chronic injury and it's not getting better after physical therapy, chiropractic, or massage, bring it up to your doctor and talk about it as a potential form of evaluation, and then go with their recommendation.

Do I have to continually see my primary care provider (PCP)?

Yes, regularly. You should see them early and then follow their advice. Schedule regular appointments to make sure that your recovery is on track. This is not only a good idea for your health, but it is also an excellent way of documenting your post-collision condition so that you can ensure you are compensated properly.

What if I do not have a primary care provider?

If you don't have one, find one close to you or one that is recommended to you as soon as you can. It is important to establish care with someone because this can be a long haul. You could be in treatment for your injuries for weeks, months, or years so it's good to establish care with a primary care physician who can "quarterback" your treatment as the extent of your injuries become known.

How often must I treat for my injuries?

It all falls back to what your primary care provider (PCP) has prescribed. If they give you 12 sessions of physical therapy to do in three months, it's in your best interest to do them. But it is important to keep checking in with your PCP as your recovery progresses to make sure you are getting the correct type of treatment and that your healing progress does not stall.

Often, we have clients who start seeing a certain type of health care provider but stop checking in with their PCP. Then all of a sudden they realize they have been treating for many months and aren't getting better, or perhaps they had some positive benefit in the first few weeks of treatment but progress has been stalled for some time. Often automobile collision victims get benefits from chiropractic treatment between the first two and three months following a collision, but after that, they are doing more maintenance than curative treatment. To make matters worse, at that point, the PIP money may be gone, and they can't afford to pay for the next step in the treatment.

That's why it's important to be checking in with your PCP. They should be at the top of the pyramid so that they can advise you of the most effective and efficient treatment available given your unique circumstances.

Should I make an appointment with my chiropractor?

Ideally, you would go to your doctor first, and get their recommendation. If you see your chiropractor first, an insurance adjuster could use that to say you had a pre-existing condition that was not caused by the collision. If you go to your doctor first, and they refer you to a chiropractor, you will start a brand new file and it won't be on the record that you went to him before.

You can make an appointment with any treatment provider you wish. Our recommendation is to always make an appointment with your primary care physician and follow their advice regarding any treatment they prescribe. You can discuss your chiropractic, physical therapy, massage, and acupuncture treatment with your primary care physician and together create a plan for your best recovery. If you have already started treatment with your chiropractor, it is wise to check in with your primary care physician.

Who do I contact if I had a concussion?

Talk to your PCP if you are noticing symptoms of a concussion. If you are unsure what to do, talk to your attorney. We know what to look for in these types of cases because we have dealt with so many of them. As the science behind traumatic brain injuries improves, we as attorneys are better able to prove that mood and behavioral changes were caused by the collision, so it is important for our clients to take note of and document those symptoms. We can also make recommendations on what specialists to see, so you can get the best treatment, and make sure it is covered by your insurance.

Dealing with injuries and documenting those injuries through proper medical treatment is a very serious matter. By now, you see why some people make a big mistake by not listening to their primary care provider or following up properly with their treatment and obtaining the documentation that accompanies it. In the next chapter, we are going to cover how you are going to pay for your treatment so that you maximize your rights and potential benefits.

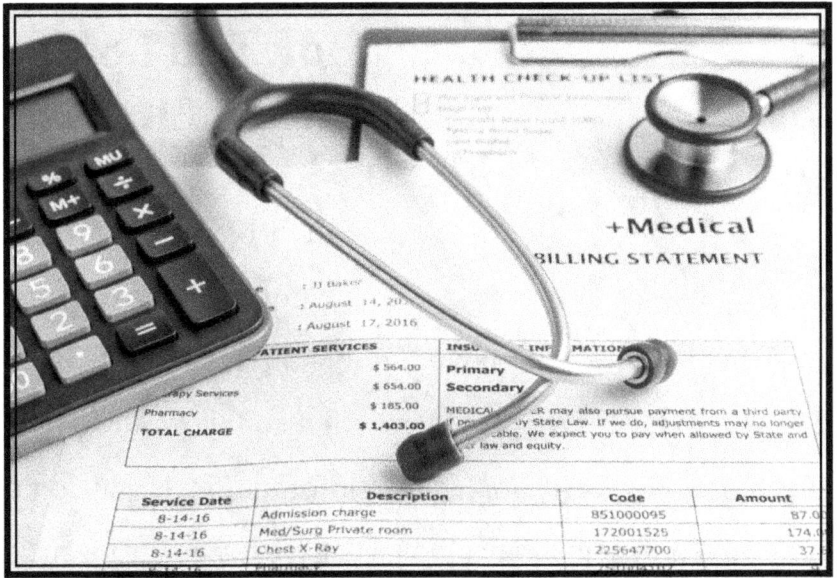

Chapter 4: Paying For Treatment

In this chapter, we discuss health Insurance, PIP coverage, Medicare and Medicaid, alternative methods of payment, crime victims compensation, and L&I, all of which can seriously impact how you ultimately pay for your treatment.

How will I pay for the ER visit?

Your PIP coverage will pay for collision-related healthcare until that coverage exhausts, usually after $10,000. Health care providers will also take your health insurance, Medicare, or Medicaid information. If you don't have any form of insurance, you will have to pay the medical bills yourself after your PIP exhausts. Usually, the best way to do this is by setting up a payment plan.

Attorneys can often get the healthcare provider to hold the bill until the time of settlement. That way the bill can be paid out of the settlement, instead of out of your pocket.

Who pays my medical bills?

If you have PIP, it will pay first. If you don't, or it is all used up, your physician should bill your health insurance. However, because it is a car crash, they may not want to pay and will instead assume you have PIP paying your bills. This is when the process gets complicated, and we as your attorneys will handle it for you.

Do I have Personal Injury Protection (PIP) insurance?

The rule in Washington is that you have PIP unless you waived it by signing a waiver. Interestingly, we've had cases where our clients called their insurance and they didn't have PIP. So we called their insurance and asked for the signed declaration waiving PIP, and they couldn't come up with it. If the insurance company cannot provide the PIP waiver, they must provide those benefits to you.

How do I bill to my PIP?

Call your insurance company or broker, and let them know that you were in a collision and need to use your PIP. They will assign you a claim number, which you will give to your care providers, along with the name of your insurance company and your adjuster's contact information.

Will my doctor take PIP?

Most therapists and doctors will take PIP. Sometimes a doctor's office will bill you directly if they don't take PIP. In this case, PIP will reimburse you once you give the bill to your insurance adjuster. This is why it is important to have good documentation. It can get complicated, so you want to have all the paperwork necessary to make sure you can get paid.

How much is my PIP?

PIP is usually pretty cheap for the amount of coverage you get. The cost varies, but it will be listed on the declarations page of your insurance policy. The coverage is usually $10,000, but it can be up to $35,000. We recommend using PIP because it covers the cost of everything up to the limit on your policy, like copays. There are often other benefits to PIP, as well. For instance, there could be a wage loss component where PIP will pay a portion of your lost wages. PIP may also pay for essential duties around the house if you can't complete them, like lawn care or cleaning services. If you don't use PIP and use your health insurance instead, you won't get these added benefits and will have to pay your deductible, which can get very expensive. As your attorneys, we can often reduce the amount of money you have to pay back to the PIP carrier at the end of the claim, which means more compensation to you.

What if I don't have PIP or health insurance?

If you don't have PIP or health insurance, you will have to pay out of pocket. This will get very expensive, so it is a good idea to get an attorney because we can set up treatment on a lien basis. We can work with health care providers who may be willing to treat you and wait for payment until your injury claim has been settled.

Who pays my copays and deductibles?

There are no copays or deductibles when using PIP. If you don't have PIP and instead are using your health insurance, you will have to pay these expenses. However, as part of your claim, you will get reimbursed by the at-fault party for all of your medical expenses, which includes amounts that have gone to copays and deductibles.

Do I have to pay back my insurance?

Yes, you do, but it is paid directly out of the settlement of your injury claim. We will negotiate to make that repayment as low as possible so you can keep as much of your compensation as possible. The money you save on repayment all goes back to you.

Why is my health insurance refusing to pay for treatments?

PIP is the primary insurance for car collisions, and your health insurance expects that you have it because under Washington state law it is required unless you waived it. This means that unless you can prove to your health insurance that you do not have PIP, or that it has been used up, they will not pay.

You have to be careful here because we see cases where the medical provider bills to our client's health insurance, but they refuse to pay because it was a car collision. This is all happening behind the scenes, and the client thinks that everything has been taken care of until they get a collections notice. Then they have to scramble to get out of collections so a lawsuit isn't filed against them! This is another example of the complexities involved in making an injury claim after a collision and why hiring an attorney is so important.

How do I keep my bills out of collections?

The best way is to communicate well, which is something we as your attorneys are very good at. We will make sure that your bills are being paid and never sent to collections. Often, people think that the at-fault driver's insurance should pay, which is true, but they don't pay as you go. They only pay after the claim has been settled, meaning that you or your insurance will have to pay in the meantime. However, an increasingly accepted method of payment in the industry is a letter of guarantee from an attorney, which says the health care provider will be paid in full out of the settlement agreement once the claim has been settled.

What if my chiropractor or physical therapist I am using does not take my health insurance?

Most treatment providers are very happy to take PIP insurance. If you do not have PIP, and your health care provider does not accept your medical insurance, talk to your attorney about working with your doctor or therapist to provide services on a lien basis, or to guarantee payment to them after the claim is settled using a letter of guarantee.

What if I cannot afford my health insurance deductible?

Your attorney can help you come up with options on how to keep your bills out of collection while you treat for your injuries. We can help you set up a payment plan or give the health care provider a letter of guarantee. The last resort is to take out a loan to pay it. We have helped our clients do this before in extreme cases, and it is an option, but a rare occurrence as we are pretty skilled at finding other options. If you have a strong injury claim, we can usually convince treatment providers to hold the bills and get paid at the time of settlement.

What if I do not have health insurance or PIP coverage?

Your attorney can help you find a therapist or doctor who will take your case on a lien basis or a letter of guarantee. There is a statute that allows a healthcare provider to file a lien at the courthouse, this is a complicated process, and is one we try to avoid but will do if necessary. The other option is to give them a letter of guarantee that simply states that you direct your attorney to pay the healthcare provider directly out of any settlement or verdict that you may achieve.

Will my insurance rates go up if I use my PIP?

Your insurance rates should not go up by simply using your PIP benefits. PIP is considered no-fault insurance, so it doesn't matter who caused the collision. In fact, even if you are totally at fault for a collision, you still can use your PIP to pay for medical care! However, any time you are at fault for a collision, you run the risk of an increased insurance premium down the road.

Which insurance would be best to use?

If you have PIP coverage, you will be required to use PIP first, because it is the most comprehensive coverage and is considered the primary coverage under Washington law. Secondary payers would be health insurance, Medicare, Medicaid, and the VA if you are a veteran.

Sometimes there are multiple PIP coverages that you can use. For example, if you are a passenger in a car that gets hit, you can use the PIP coverage on your personal policy and the PIP coverage of the insurance on the car in which you were a passenger. Another example is if a vehicle hits a pedestrian, that pedestrian gets the PIP benefit of the vehicle that hit them and then potentially their own PIP benefit if they have their own automobile insurance policy.

It is our job to carefully read *all* applicable insurance policies to make sure you maximize your PIP benefits and leave no benefits behind that might help pay for medical treatment.

Why doesn't the automobile insurance for the person who hit me pay my medical bills?

They do, but they only pay those medical bills when you settle your injury claim. That means we have to find ways to help you pay your medical bills until the claim settles. Your claim should only be presented to the at-fault driver's insurance company in its entirety after you are done treating. If you settle it before you are done treating, then you are leaving money on the table by not making the insurance company pay all your medical bills. There is no legal mechanism to compel them to pay your bills as you treat. This is because the insurance companies would only send you to their approved doctors, who would treat you as quickly as possible and try to get you to stop treatment early in order to save the insurance company money. In short, you only get "one bite at the apple" so you must be fully healed and done with treatment before we can settle your claim for you.

Even after you have settled your claim, the insurance company will try to hold onto their money as long as they can. It is our job to get that money for you, and we are good at it. Once the claim is settled, the settlement amount goes into a Trust Account, which will pay the bills you have accrued. The Trust Account is managed by the Washington State Bar Association.

Now that you have an understanding regarding how to get your medical treatment paid, let's take a look at fortifying your injury claim. The next discussion will explain approaching settlements, how you can make sure you have a consistent track record of following through with treatment so your medical documentation becomes an impenetrable fortress and you can settle your claim with the best possible outcome.

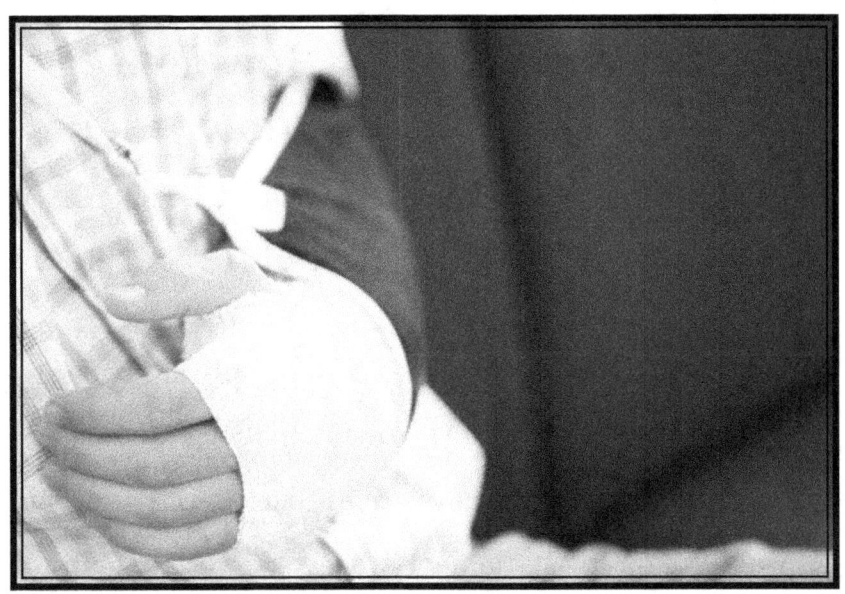

Chapter 5: Settlements—Why You Need To Follow Through And Be Consistent With Your Treatment

In this chapter, we cover the process steps in a settlement, the importance of making and keeping medical treatment appointments, why checking in with primary care physicians is so important, how medications play a role, what to do about referrals, and how to make sure you have no gaps in your treatment.

How do I know when it is time to settle?

We recommend you do not settle anything until after you are completely done with your treatment and your doctor says that you probably won't have any setbacks. At that point, we would begin the settlement process. Many people think it is okay to settle while they are still in treatment with the expectation they will have a full and complete recovery. However, if your recovery goes slower or has setbacks, you cannot "unring the bell" if you settle your claim early.

We always recommend you wait until your doctors and therapists have discharged you from any further treatment. At that point, we would assess your recovery to determine if you are close to 100% recovered or if you feel like you have reached maximum medical improvement. If you are 100% recovered, we can feel confident in moving forward with a settlement. If you are only 75% recovered, then we would likely need to get a statement from your treatment provider(s) about any further treatment you might need, how long a full recovery might be if at all, and how much money future treatment might cost. At that point, we would have all the evidence and would try to place a value on your claim to bring to the insurance company.

Will they pressure me to settle?

The other driver's insurance company will *always* pressure you to settle early. They want to close the claim as cheaply as possible, and as quickly as they can. Unfortunately, we frequently speak with clients who regret settling a collision injury claim before they were fully healed.

We want our clients to be thorough with their treatment and be open and honest with their doctors. We do not want to settle the claim until they know they are either better or as good as they are going to get. Even if there is any residual pain, we can include that with what we demand in the settlement.

What happens if I settle too soon?

Sometimes clients will come to us having already settled, whether it was because of the pressure from the insurance adjuster or a personal financial issue, and they will ask us what we can do because they realized they were more injured than they initially thought. We have had cases in the past where we have been able to reopen the claim and renegotiate the settlement after further treatment, but it is difficult to undo a release and we never recommend settling with an insurance company before treatment is complete. If you ever have any doubts, call an attorney at our firm. We will give you our best advice regarding your options.

Is it too late to use my Personal Injury Protection (PIP)?

In Washington, there is a three-year statute of limitations on personal injury cases. The three year period allows you to use and take advantage of your PIP benefits in that time frame. By contrast, in Oregon, you only have one year by law to use any or all of your PIP benefits. Having PIP benefits is a contractual legal matter between you and your insurance company, so it depends on what state you were in when you purchased your insurance contract to determine which statute applies to your PIP benefits.

Should I go to the "Independent" Medical Exam (IME) my insurance company has set up for me?

In certain circumstances, your insurance company will require that you attend a medical examination performed by a physician of their choosing, in order to receive PIP benefits. You signed a contract with your insurance company, which means you have duties to each other. You have a duty to cooperate with your insurance company and attend the medical examination. Your insurance company has a duty to provide you with the benefits you paid for.

Regardless of what the insurance company says, the IME is being scheduled because your insurance company, for whatever reason, has questions about whether your current treatment is reasonable and necessary. The insurance company will send you to a doctor who will often deem you to be fixed and stable, or to have reached maximum medical improvement. The insurance doctor will then recommend you undergo no further treatment and the insurance company will not pay for any further treatment. In short, the examination is not independent in any way and is designed to allow the insurance company to improperly avoid paying your medical expenses.

We do many things to combat this. One is to have you go to your primary care physician shortly before or after the IME appointment and discuss the IME exam with them in order to be able to give greater weight to your personal doctor's notes over the insurance company's physician. We can also go get statements from your medical treatment providers to send to your insurance company to show the IME doctor. Sometimes efforts change the IME doctor's position. If it does not, additional legal remedies may exist for you.

Why do I need to see a Primary Care Physician (PCP)?

Your PCP will be able to "quarterback" your medical treatment. Typically, people have a medical doctor they know and trust who is familiar with their medical history. That is the first place we send people to get evaluated. Your PCP can recommend the best type of care for you and monitor your treatment throughout your recovery. Generally, your PCP is also the most credentialed and qualified professional to make a statement supporting your treatment and care.

Why do I need to keep treating if it does not seem to help?

Medical treatment is difficult. It can take a long time. It is painful and inconvenient, but completing your prescribed treatment is *critically* important to your recovery if that is what your doctor recommends. There are a couple reasons for this. One, while treatment is long and tedious, there is a point where you do start feeling better, so please do not give up. Second, you need to have a documented paper trail showing that you completed and followed through with all of your recommended and prescribed treatments, otherwise the insurance company will try to minimize your settlement by arguing you did not comply with your doctor's treatment recommendation.

If you really believe your treatment is not working, talk to your treatment providers about it. They will likely either agree with you or recommend other treatment modalities for you.

Should I fill the prescriptions for pain medications given to me by my doctor?

Prescription drugs are like everything else: they are a type of treatment the doctor believes would be beneficial for you to cope with the pain you are in. But with any prescription medications, there are side effects or addiction concerns that may cause you to not want to fill those prescriptions. You should discuss these concerns with your doctor.

Do I need to go to the referrals my doctor gives me?

You definitely need to go to the type of treatment(s) they recommend, but you do not have to go to the specific treatment provider they recommend. You can choose who you want to work with. Location and proximity to where you live or work will play a large role in whether or not you will be able to consistently follow up and attend all your visits. When deciding what treatment providers to work with, consider these factors: location, quality of care and service, reputation, and whether or not you feel comfortable with the treatment provider.

Should I go back to the doctor if I have new pain?

Yes, you should definitely report any new pain to your doctor. Clients who initially experience knee and ankle pain after a collision months later may notice they acquired back pain because their manner of walking from the initial injuries has changed and created new back pain. This is common, and you should talk to your doctor about it because they can diagnose it as related to the collision, and we can incorporate that into your injury claim. Be sure to notify all of your treatment providers when you notice new symptoms.

What if I stopped treatment for a few months but still have pain?

We never like to see a gap in treatment. A gap in treatment is always going to be an opportunity for the at-fault driver's insurance company to deny your claim. They will argue something else caused new pain or you stopped treatment because the pain was never really too bad. Nevertheless, your treatment and condition is the number one priority. If you are still hurting, go to the doctor and let your attorney deal with the insurance company problems.

Should I go back to my PCP for referrals to my therapist when my prescription runs out?

Yes. It is important to keep checking with your doctor because they will be able to tell if the treatment is working. We often see clients get stuck in a treatment mode, going to the chiropractor or physical therapist for months, even after their recoveries plateau. Your doctor will be able to determine your recovery and refer you for continued care with your current treatment or provide alternative treatment options.

How long should I be doing this treatment?

You should do the prescribed treatment for as long as your doctor or treatment provider recommends. If the treatment is not helping solve the root problem and is only treating the symptoms, you might want to look into another form of treatment. Many times the treatment you are doing eventually only helps relieve your pain for a short time period, like a day or so, and does not provide a long-term solution for recovery. Always stay in touch with your PCP and other treatment providers and follow their recommended treatment plan.

What if I do not have time to keep going to treatment?

It will impact the value of your claim if you stop treatment prematurely, but there might be other avenues you could explore, such as treating less often. For instance, if you cannot attend treatment twice a week, go once a week. Then, not only are you doing something to treat yourself, you are also providing chart notes and medical records that can be used as evidence showing you are still hurt and doctors are still actively trying to help you recover. If you cannot treat at all, be sure to check in with your PCP, because they can document the reasons you are unable to treat, such as, "patient is inundated with children, two jobs, and a personal issue and is unable to treat at this time. I am prescribing medication and will follow up in three weeks." That communication gives us the supportive evidence we need to explain why you are unable to treat or have a gap in your treatment.

Can I go to a therapist or a chiropractor closer to my home or work?

Yes, convenience is very important. If the treatment is inconvenient to you, it is harder to complete treatment. Getting treatment is the most important thing you can do, and you are entitled to go wherever you need to in order to get treatment. If there is no PIP available and you are using your health insurance to pay for your medical care, you will be limited by the network of providers in your health insurance policy. Contact your health insurance to determine what treatment locations are near you.

You now understand how important it is to have a PCP as one of the key members of your recovery team. They are like your quarterback and are a very important part of documenting your claim for a good outcome, in terms of your recovery and the amount of settlement money you receive. Now that you have a thorough understanding of following through with your treatment, let's explore the actual demand package itself and how you can settle your claim so you can get paid and get back to normal again.

Chapter 6: Getting Compensation By Using A Strong Demand Package

In this chapter, we focus on staying proactive with a demand package. In addition, we cover the various details that might affect this stage of your claim so that you have the best possible chance of compensation, getting the recovery and justice you deserve, and finally get back to normal living again.

The demand package is the heart of your negotiation with the insurance company. It should include all of the evidence you wish to use to prove your claims. This evidence typically includes items such as medical records, medical bills, wage loss documentation, receipts for out of pocket expenses, the police report, vehicle repair estimates, and photographs of the vehicles and collision scene. The demand package should also include a narrative description of how the collision occurred, the highlights of your medical treatment, and a detailed description of how the collision and the resulting injuries have impacted your life.

How much is my injury worth?

You never truly know what your claim is worth at the beginning. There are a lot of factors that go into it. We tell clients that we need to analyze many factors such as the types of injuries they suffered, the duration of medical treatment, the long-term issues they are left with after treatment has stopped, liability problems, the force of the impact generated in the collision, and how pre-existing injuries or conditions may play into a potential settlement.

The most important factor in determining settlement value, however, is the type of injury you've suffered. We generally tell people there are three broad categories. The first is a soft tissue type of injury where you treat for several months with physical therapy and chiropractors and make a good recovery. The second type is when the recovery is a little bit more stubborn and you might have to get an MRI or be referred to a specialist for epidural steroid injections or something similar. The third category has the largest amount of damages and is typically characterized by the need for surgical intervention. Those are the three broad categories, but we don't know the value until you're done treating and your demand letter is done.

What is a "Demand Package?"

The "demand package," also called a "demand letter," is what we send to the insurance company to start negotiations. It has all the evidence that we've gathered in the case, police reports, photos, witness statements, medical records, and medical bills. In other words, it describes who's to blame, how the collision happened, what type of medical treatment and expenses you incurred, and how much you feel you deserve in compensation.

It is a thorough package because we are trying to produce a package of information that we can use readily in litigation if needed. So, if we are forced to file a lawsuit, much of the work is already done. This is important because the insurance company will know we're ready to file a lawsuit and go to trial if needed. We are often able to get more money for our clients than other firms because of our thorough preparation. The insurance company doesn't want to go to trial because they know we are serious about the case from the beginning, which makes a reasonable settlement before a lawsuit more likely.

How long does it take to get a settlement?

This is a difficult question to answer because there are so many variables, the most important of which is the duration of your treatment. We typically need to wait until your treatment has concluded in order to have a full understanding of your damages and claim value.

Generally speaking, once treatment is done we order the medical records, put the demand letter together, and send it to the insurance company. Thirty days is a reasonable amount of time for the insurance company to analyze the demand materials and present an offer of settlement. So, after your treatment ends, it can take two to three months to fully prepare and finalize the demand letter, another month for the insurance company to analyze it and present an offer, and another four to six weeks to negotiate with the insurance adjuster. Most claims are settled at that point. However, every claim is different and the amount of time needed to settle the claim varies widely. Further, if the claim cannot be settled, we will commence litigation and a new time estimate for resolving the claim would be given after consultation with your attorney.

What is the process now that I'm done with treatment and how does settlement work?

Once you're done treating, we have a conversation with you and make sure that we know all of the treatment providers that you saw during the course of your treatment. We then order the medical records and put together the demand letter. The medical records typically take four to six weeks to get once we order them; once we have those, it will usually take us about a month to draft the demand letter and a month for the insurance company to evaluate the claim. In creating the demand letter, we dig deep into the medical records to make sure nothing is missed. We are vigilant to make sure that all of your expenses and bills are accounted for, such as "behind the scenes" bills like imaging, labs, and medications. We find these to ensure they aren't sent to collections, and also so we can make sure they make it into the demand letter so that you ultimately achieve as much compensation as possible.

At this point, we also double check with all of your health care providers to make sure we know of any outstanding balances that may exist and need to be paid, and contact any health insurance company that paid any bill related to the injuries you sustained in the collision. Under the law, even insurance companies may have a legal right to be paid back a portion of what is collected from your settlement, so we want to make sure everything is paid off in full at the time your settlement is finalized so that you have no surprises down the road.

What happens if a medical provider has a lien against me?

Sometimes a health care provider will file a lien as an additional layer of security to ensure that they receive payment. Once we settle your claim and pay them, they will file the paperwork with the county to remove the lien.

How do I know if I have Uninsured Motorist (UIM) coverage?

You can check with your insurance agent and you can check with your own documents. If you save your policy, it will be on the declarations page which is usually included with a copy of your policy. It also might be on the insurance card that you keep in your car. We recommend that everyone have UIM and PIP.

Do I need to give the insurance company my medical records from before the motor vehicle collision?

No, you don't have to. The insurance company may want to devalue your claim by claiming your collision-related injuries were actually pre-existing injuries. If they see you had shoulder pain a year ago, they might argue that the collision did not cause your current pain, which will diminish the value of your claim. We tell people not to sign anything, because usually, the insurance company will ask you to sign a form which will give them access to all of your medical records, both related to the current collision and any old unrelated records you may have with your healthcare provider. Often people sign these documents without realizing the ramifications because they think it is just part of the process. If this happens and we are hired to represent you, we send the insurance company a letter saying all previous authorizations are revoked.

How does the insurance company come up with a value for my injury claim?

For the past 15-plus years, insurance companies have relied on software to guide them in settling claims. The insurance adjuster will plug in relevant information such as diagnostic and billing codes, and the computer will give a settlement range. Often, a lawsuit or the threat of a lawsuit will allow the insurance adjuster to go beyond the computer-generated range and settle the claim for an amount that is fair.

Do I get my medical records?

We do that for you. You don't want to because often the health care provider does not give you everything, and you may not know what to look for when requesting the records. We need to make sure that we have access to the most comprehensive set of records available because we rely on them as the foundation of your claim.

Do I need to provide unrelated medical records?

That's for your attorney to decide and it's an important decision. If it's unrelated, then no, and we have a good sense of what might be related and what isn't. There may be times when we do release unrelated records in an effort to show that you had no similar pain or injuries in the past. Again, this is an issue that is best decided with your attorney during the course of negotiating your claim.

Will I get reimbursed for my lost wages?

Yes, be sure to get a doctor's note on the timeframe that you're claiming for lost wages. Be ready to help us get your employment records to prove that timeframe along with how much you were paid, how much you lost in potential overtime, and how many sick or personal days you had to use to cover your time off. The doctor's note is very important because it is proof that you took work off because it was medically necessary, and not for some other reason.

Will I get my gas money back for traveling to appointments?

If you keep track of it, we can claim it.

Do I need to pay back my insurance company?

This is a very complex area of law that you will likely spend much time on with your attorney. Generally speaking, under the law you do have to pay back your insurance company for benefits they paid on your behalf, such as for paying medical bills. However, there are a number of legal arguments your attorney can make in order to reduce this amount, or even get it waived altogether.

Why do I have to repay my insurance?

You have to pay back your insurance because if you don't you get a double benefit. This would consist of having your medical bills paid along with collecting money for your medical expenses from the settlement. Typically we can negotiate the repayment cost down, and under some circumstances get it waived altogether. The less you have to repay, the more compensation stays with you.

What if I do not want to pay medical bills that are outstanding?

Typically you must pay outstanding medical bills because there is a signed agreement in place saying you will, in order for the health care provider to provide the service. They may want your attorney to sign a letter of guarantee or they may also file a lien. However, everything is open to negotiation. We try as hard as we can to reduce the amount our clients have to pay out of their settlement, and we can often reduce the amount owed by a substantial amount.

Do I have to pay taxes on my settlement?

Typically no. The only part you have to pay taxes on is any part of your settlement that goes to wage loss. Typically the release documentation is worded in such a way so that there is no resultant tax liability. If the settlement funds are for pain and suffering or medical expenses, they are tax-free.

Now that you have a settlement and the light can be seen at the end of the tunnel, you are almost done ... but not quite. There are a few lingering questions that we have to answer about the post-settlement process so that you can finally move on with your life as quickly and easily as possible.

Chapter 7: Post Settlement— What To Do After The Dust Settles

In this chapter, we cover what happens after your settlement is complete. This includes releases, tax implications if you had wage loss, your investment options, structured settlements, who pays after the settlement, and UIM claims. You want to make sure you dot all your I's and cross all your T's, and this chapter will help you do just that.

Is there other insurance to tap into?

There could be. First, we look at the liability insurance of the person who hit you. Then we look at UIM coverage on your own policy. There may be other potential sources of insurance or compensation for you as well, depending on the unique circumstances of your case. For example, if the at-fault driver is working for a business, we look to see if the company has a liability policy on the company vehicle.

Can I get money or assets from the wrongdoer?

You can, but it is difficult. Generally, if the at-fault driver has no insurance they are not likely to be independently wealthy and therefore available assets are limited and difficult to make a claim on before they file for bankruptcy. Once they file for bankruptcy, the claim could be dischargeable in court, meaning you won't be able to get anything from them. We may employ the services of an investigator to find out if the at-fault driver has substantial assets from which to pay a settlement or verdict. A release of the at-fault driver should not be signed if you think you may want to pursue the personal assets of the wrongdoer.

What if I aggravate an injury in the future?

When the release document is signed and you get your settlement, the claim is closed forever. We want our clients to realize this so they don't rush their settlement. We want to make sure that they are as healthy as possible to make sure we cover everything in the claim. If there is any residual pain we will build that into the settlement.

Who pays for future medical bills?

That can be built into the settlement, but we need to have good evidence of what the future medical bills will look like. If we have good medical evidence of the need for the future treatment we can make a viable claim for the value of the future treatment.

Can I put my settlement into an annuity?

Yes, you can. Typically this only makes sense with larger settlements. We can make recommendations on who to meet for advice with financial issues such as this. Putting settlement funds into financial products can be a good option for minors and those with disabilities as well.

Why do I have to sign a release?

You have to sign a release prior to an insurance company paying you the money from the settlement. They want to make sure the case is closed and you can't come back in the future for more money.

How long does it take to receive my check?

It usually takes around three weeks once you sign the release. The release is sent to the insurance company, and once it is received by the insurance company they will issue and send the settlement check. Once the settlement check is received by your attorney's office it will go into a trust account for a sufficient amount of time to make sure the check clears.

Conclusion

Now that you know exactly what to do after being in a collision, including navigating the complex medical and insurance systems, getting paid, getting your car fixed, and getting back to normal, you can choose a law firm who will be your partner so that you can breathe easy and live life again. We can help you settle your injury claim and would be happy to assist you.

If you are like most people, we are guessing that what you have read here probably opened your eyes to things you never thought of before. If you are unsure that you want to go forward with handling your own claim, we want to offer you a free, no-pressure, initial consultation. Let us help get this all behind you. If you are ready to tackle the legal problem and need help with the insurance companies after a collision, the team at Russell & Hill is ready to go to work for you. Simply visit us at www.RussellAndHill.com or call **1-800-LAW-0842** for a free consultation.

Glossary of Terms

There are several terms that might be unfamiliar to you as you read through this book. Please refer to this glossary of terms, which are provided here, in alphabetical order:

Adjuster

An insurance adjuster is an employee of an insurance company who handles an evaluates a claim. Insurance adjusters are incentivized to avoid paying claims.

At-Fault Driver

The at-fault driver is the driver or drivers in a collision who caused the collision and will be legally liable for injuries and damages they cause.

Automobile Accident/Collision/ Crash

We use these terms somewhat interchangeably in our daily lives. When it comes to making an injury claim after an automobile collision, we do not believe the appropriate description to use is "accident." Driving a vehicle safely is a relatively easy task. Nearly all automobile collisions are caused because someone was not driving safely or following the rules of the road. We use the term collision to properly describe an automobile crash.

Claim

We use the term *claim* to describe all the ways you will present your request for benefits or compensation after being injured in a collision. You may make a claim for medical coverage to your own insurance company. You may make a claim for vehicle damage to your own or another person's insurance company. You may make a claim for compensatory damages to the insurance company of a person who has injured you.

Consultation

A consultation is the initial discussion of your case with an attorney or case manager. Our firm offers a free, no-pressure, consultation to discuss your collision and all the issues related to it. We can do this via phone, video-conference, or in person. We even make house calls from time to time!

Contingency Fee

Our law firm represents injury clients on a contingency fee basis. That means you pay us our attorney fee as a percentage of the settlement of your injury claim. The contingency fee approach allows persons of all income levels to have access to justice. It also provides a foundation of trust in our relationship by directly aligning our fees to your recovery.

Independent Medical Examination (IME)

Your insurance company may ask for an IME in order to review your claim for PIP benefits or UIM benefits. The IME is not independent. It is not designed to fairly evaluate your injury claim. You do, however, have to participate in the IME under the terms of your insurance contract.

Insurance

In this book, we discuss several types of insurance coverage. The most important ones are defined here.

First-Party Insurance

This is your own insurance or insurance you may otherwise be directly covered by. By law, insurance companies are duty-bound to handle first-party coverages different than third-party coverages. Examples of first-party coverages are UIM (uninsured/underinsured motorist) and PIP (personal injury protection).

UIM

Uninsured or Underinsured Motorist Coverage is a type of first-party coverage that covers damages in the event you are injured by a person who has no insurance or insufficient insurance. To make a claim under your UIM policy, you must prove that an uninsured/underinsured person was at fault for the injuries you suffered in the collision.

PIP

Personal Injury Protection insurance provides coverage for medical expenses (and possibly other types of damage) arising from the collision. PIP is "no-fault" coverage, which means that you do not need to prove another vehicle caused the collision in order to receive PIP benefits.

Third-Party Insurance

This is the insurance that covers the at-fault driver.

Letter Of Guarantee

In certain circumstances, your attorneys can provide a letter of guarantee to your medical treatment providers so that they will continue to provide treatment without immediate payment. The letter of guarantee ensures the medical treatment provider that their bills will be paid from the injury claim settlement.

Lien

A *Lien* is a right to keep possession of property belonging to another person until a debt owed by that person is discharged. There are many types of liens and this is a term you are likely familiar with. In this book, lien refers to one filed by a medical treatment provider with the Court. The goal for the medical treatment provider is to ensure payment of outstanding medical expenses from the injury claim settlement.

Litigation

Unfortunately, some injury claims cannot be settled with the insurance company, for various reasons. In that event, we will have to file a lawsuit to protect your rights. Once the lawsuit is filed, we call this phase litigation. We attempt to avoid litigation, but it is sometimes required.

Policy Limits

Each type of insurance coverage extends only to a specific dollar figure. These are the "limits" of an insurance coverage or policy. In Washington, drivers are required to carry $25,000 in third-party insurance coverage.

Pre-Existing Condition

This is a condition, injury, or illness that exists prior to a collision. Insurance companies will always point to any condition, injury, or illness which occurred prior to a collision as the cause of post-collision symptoms.

Property (Vehicle) Damage

When your vehicle is damaged in a collision, the industry term for that type of damage is property damage. In this book, we refer to property damage as "vehicle" damage. In short, it is the physical damage caused to your vehicle in a collision.

Release

At the time of settlement of your injury claim, the at-fault driver's insurance company will require that you sign a document called a release. A release is a contract in which you exchange the settlement funds for an agreement to release your claims against the at-fault driver.

Statute Of Limitations

Specific laws govern the timeframe after a collision in which you must resolve your injury claim or file a lawsuit. In Washington, you have three years from the time of the collision to resolve the claim or you must file a lawsuit.

Total-Loss

The common phrase for a total-loss vehicle is that the vehicle was "totaled" or "totaled out" by an insurance company. Typically, this means that the insurance company evaluating the damage has determined that the cost to repair a vehicle is 80% or more of the market value of the vehicle.

About The Authors

James V. Hill

Jim grew up in Lynnwood, Washington, in the Martha Lake area. He attended Washington State University for his undergraduate degree before attending Seattle University to obtain his law degree. While at WSU he met his wife Pam, and they now have 3 kids aged 11, 14 and 16. Outside of work, Jim coaches the Junior Olympic running team and enjoys supporting his kids in their endeavors. He is an active runner and enjoys racing in marathons and Ragnar relays.

Matthew T. Russel

Matt grew up in a rural small town in Southeast Minnesota. He was an avid hunter and enjoyed playing football, basketball, and golf. After high school Matt attended Clemson University in South Carolina for his undergraduate degree and went on to earn his J.D. Degree at Hamline University School of Law in 2000 in St. Paul, MN. After graduation, Matt and his wife Carolyn moved to the Maple leaf area in North Seattle, and Matt opened an office in Bellevue. Matt and Carolyn now live in rural Snohomish County with their four children, ages 10-15 at the time of this publishing. Matt enjoys coaching youth basketball, mock trial and is active on the School Board and is on the Board of Mercy Watch, an outreach program for the homeless in Snohomish County. Matt loves his work and cherishes his family and friends, and continues to strive always to be a better attorney, father, and husband.

I really don't like CO2.

It warms the earth

and sticks like glue.

And whether it's old
or whether it's new,

we've all got a
problem with CO2!

Now some people aren't sure if it's true:

all this talk about CO2.

But just between me
and you,

We know **all about** **CO2!**

If we want the sky
to keep its blue,

and we don't want
the rivers

to resemble a stew,

then we need to
reduce our CO2,

and think about this
problem anew.

If you've been wondering what to do,

about this issue
called CO2,

you better sit down

and think it through

before you continue
with CO2.

I really don't like CO2.

It isn't good for me
or you.

It's spewing from
factories night and
day,

and in the end, we all have to pay!

Our cars are expelling all that stuff,

and now the
weather's way too
rough.

Do you really know
what you do

when you keep
emitting CO2?

Daily we see the climate change,

and the earth itself
will rearrange.

We need to cut our oil and coal

if we want the earth

to still remain
whole.

At least we have the trees in line.

They love the CO2,
and that's fine.

But trees alone
won't heal our
sphere.

For that, we'll have to begin right here.

Our planet's suffering right now,

and we all want to
fix it,

but the question is
how?!

We ought to be thinking about a solution

before our Earth's
overrun by
pollution!

The fuel of fossils is near an end,

and a brand-new world

is around the bend.

You better call your leaders quick

and see if they have
a trick

to stop the global
warming now

or we'll all be suffering,

and how!!!

www.ingramcontent.com/pod-product-compliance
Lightning Source LLC
Chambersburg PA
CBHW071243220526
45468CB00002B/979